Thomas Hugo

The last ten Years of the Priory of S. Helen, Bishopsgate, in

the City of London

With the Topography of that House

Thomas Hugo

The last ten Years of the Priory of S. Helen, Bishopsgate, in the City of London
With the Topography of that House

ISBN/EAN: 9783337107321

Printed in Europe, USA, Canada, Australia, Japan

Cover: Foto ©ninafisch / pixelio.de

More available books at **www.hansebooks.com**

THE LAST TEN YEARS

OF THE

PRIORY OF S. HELEN, BISHOPSGATE,

IN THE CITY OF LONDON;

WITH

THE TOPOGRAPHY OF THAT HOUSE.

BY

THOMAS HUGO, M.A., F.S.A., F.R.S.L.,

HONORARY SECRETARY OF THE LONDON AND MIDDLESEX ARCHÆOLOGICAL
SOCIETY,

&c. &c. &c.

LONDON:
PRINTED BY NICHOLS AND SONS,
25, PARLIAMENT STREET.

1865.

THE LAST TEN YEARS

PRIORY OF S. HELEN, BISHOPSGATE,

IN THE CITY OF LONDON,

WITH THE TOPOGRAPHY OF THAT HOUSE.

In mediæval times the City of London and its suburbs contained a number of Houses of Religious Women, among which were conspicuous, both for their architectural excellence and the value of their possessions, those of Clerkenwell, Stratford-le-Bow, Halliwell, S. Helen, and the Minoresses. The annals of each of these communities are full of interest, and deserve a very different amount of attention from that which they have hitherto received. The reader will not therefore, as I suppose, be sorry to be introduced to a history of the last ten years of one of these establishments,—of which, I may add, the particulars already given to the press are of a very meagre and unsatisfactory character,—as well as to what can be gathered of its architecture and topography. I select the individual House, from its special interest for London archæologists, while the length of the interval to which I wish to give attention is limited, from a desire to impart to its investigation that fulness of detail which my space would not allow me to apply to the consecutive periods of its entire history.

I make no apology for the copiousness with which the facts are presented to the reader. True students of history, whether

A

sacred or secular, do not require a narrative compressed, as a free and easy critic has suggested, into the "space of a nutshell." Such details would, no doubt, be quite as voluminous as the intellect of such a reader could entertain; but other men, better and greater than he, are desirous of possessing something more really akin to the interest and importance of the subject. Mere skeleton histories of Religious Houses are already in the reader's hands, and the repetition of such, apart from being useless as a twice-told tale, would necessarily lose in value what it might gain in brevity. The particularity, then, of my information I hold to be its special excellence. Those only entertain a light opinion of such particularity " who are either indifferent to the subject itself, unconscious of their own deficiencies, or have an evil purpose to serve " in keeping others ignorant of the truth.

To introduce the reader to what I am about to offer, a very few words are needful about the earlier history of the place.

The Benedictine Priory of S. Helen, Bishopsgate, was founded about the year 1212. A Church had existed on the site of the present structure some time before the foundation of the Priory, and was granted to the Canons of S. Paul's by Ranulph, and Robert his son, as appears by an agreement given at length in Newcourt's *Repertorium*,[*] and the works of other writers. According to the terms of this instrument, which was made in the reign of Henry II., they were to retain it for their lives, at a rent of twelve pence a year, and were to appoint a third incumbent who should hold it after their decease, at a rent of two shillings a year, to the end of his life, after which event it was to determine to the Canons.[†]   On the death of these three parties, the Canons granted the right of patronage to William the son of William the Goldsmith. William obtained from Alard de Burnham, Dean of S. Paul's, permission to found a Priory for Nuns. This must have been not later than the year 1216, for the Dean departed this life on the 14th of August in that year. Stowe, Howel, Weever, and others, are in

---

[*] Vol. i. p. 363.   [†] Reg. Dec. et Cap. A. f. 32.

error, who attribute the foundation to William Basing, Dean of
S. Paul's; for, in the first place, there is no such person in the
list of those dignitaries, and, in the second, a document among
the archives of the Dean and Chapter distinctly proves that my
attribution of the good work to William fitz William is correct.*
Basing was a Sheriff of London in the second year of Edward II.,
and was a considerable benefactor, but not the founder.

In agreement with my intention expressed just now, of con-
fining myself to the history of the last ten years of this ancient
and interesting Community, I pass over its annals, although I am
in possession of some curious information belonging to various
periods, during the interim between its foundation and those
times of trouble when, like all similar establishments, it was
beginning to encounter its last trial,—when the storm was all
but bursting, which should consign it and them to the horrors of
a common catastrophe.

There are, however, one or two scraps of information connected
with earlier times which, I have reason to think, will be particularly welcome to those who live near to or are well acquainted with the place.

The Nuns endeavoured, especially during the reigns of Henry
III. and Edward I., to stop up the lane or passage through the
court of their House, from Bishopsgate Street to S. Mary-Axe.
In the thirty-third year of the former King they obtained a licence
to include a lane lying across their ground, inasmuch as it had
been found by inquest that no damage would accrue thereby to
the citizens of London. The licence was dated at Westminster,
the 24th March, 33 Henry III. 1248-9.† Some resistance, as it
appears, was made to this inclusion, for in several subsequent
inquests the jurors describe the lane as a common thoroughfare,
from the Gate of the Nuns of S. Elen to the Church of
S. Mary at Ax, called "Seint Eleyne Lane," through which
there was always in ancient times a common passage for carts and

* Reg. Dec. et Cap. A. f. 24 b.
† Pat. 33 Hen. III. m. 7.

horsemen, as well as for foot passengers.* Their obstruction was
at least partially successful, and, as such, has descended to our
own time. There is still no thoroughfare for carriages. .

Reynold Kentwode, Dean of S. Paul's (1422—1441), together
with his Chapter, made a number of Constitutions for the Nuns,
dated the 21st of June, 1439.† Many of these are extremely
curious, and furnish us with most descriptive illustrations of conventual life. I have accurately transcribed them from the original
document, now among the Cottonian Rolls, and have placed them
as an Appendix at the end of this memoir.

The names of the three Prioresses which are given by the last
editors of Dugdale, are Eleanor de Wyncestre or Winton, in the
7th and 12th of Edward III.; Alice Asshfeld, who granted a lease
to Sir John Crosby, the builder of Crosby Hall, in 1466 ;‡ and
Mary Rollesley, the last Prioress. To these I am able to add
four others, D——, Alice Wodehous, Alice Traethall, and Isabel
Stampe. The first-mentioned lady I believe to have been the
first Prioress. She addressed a petition, which I have given in
the Appendix, to Alard de Burnham, dean of S. Paul's, and
Walter Fitzwalter, archdeacon of London, in or some short time
previous to the year 1216. The second was the immediate pre-
decessor of Alice Asshfeld, and granted to Sir John Crosby a
lease of the house in which he resided when he obtained from the
latter that of the same and adjoining premises, on which he subsequently built his magnificent mansion. I presume that she re-
signed her office of Prioress, as a lady of the same name and
probably herself stands first of the eleven present and consenting
Sisters in the document of 1466. The third, Alice Traethall,
leased some premises in Birchin Lane, about which more details
will be given, to Thomas Knyght, by indenture dated the 20th
March, 13 Henry VII. 1497-8. The fourth, Isabel Stampe,
was the last Prioress but one. When she succeeded to her office
I cannot determine, nor the time of her decease or resignation;

* Rot. Hundred. i. 409, 410, 420, 425, 426, 431.   † Rot. Cott. v. 6.
‡ See the particulars in the Author's History of Crosby Hall, Transactions of the Lond. and Midd. Archæol. Soc. vol. i. p. 40.

but, as we shall see presently, she granted leases of some of her conventual property on the 3rd of December, 1512, and on the 1st of November, 1526.

The will of Elizabeth Rollesley, who would appear to be the mother of the last Prioress, is given by Madox in his *Formulare*. It was dated the 23rd August, 1513, 5 Henry VIII.; and, among other bequests, she directs: " Item; I bequeth to the Prioress and Covent of S. Elyns in London, v li. Item; I bequeth to Dame Mary, my dowter, being a Nonne of the same place, v li." Another daughter, Alice, was a Nun of Dartford, and to her was left a similar legacy.*

We will now proceed with the history of the last ten years of the House in its chronological order. I have collected the details from the Conventual Leases, the Ministers' Accounts, the Valor, the Surrenders, the Particulars for Grants, the Orders and Decrees, Pension Lists, Surveys, and other Records of the Court of Augmentations, the Patent and Originalia Rolls, and several collections of Rolls and Charters, or documents usually called by that name, &c. &c. And, although there may have been various other transactions of which no record has been preserved, the result will probably give the reader a more lively notion than that which he may already possess of some of the multifarious business which was a necessary ingredient in the life of a wealthy Religious House during its last few years of possession and power.

On the 26th January, 19th Hen. VIII. 1527-8, the Prioress, Mary Rollesley, and Convent leased to Richard Berde a tenement in the parish of S. Ethelburga, for a term of forty years, at an annual rent of xx s.†

On the 21st December, 20th Hen. VIII. 1528, they leased to Robert Nesham, citizen and baker, and Agnes his wife, one bakehouse, with appurtenances, in the parish of S. Andrew Undershafte, for a term of forty years from the following Christmas, at a yearly rent of lxxiij s. iiij d. The repairs were to be done by the farmer.‡

---

* Madox, Formulare Anglicanum, p. 440.

† Ministers' Accounts, 31-32 Hen. VIII. No. 112.

‡ London Conventual Leases, No. 24. Ministers' Accounts.

On the 20th May, 21st Hen. VIII. 1529, they leased to Richard Staverton a tenement in the parish of S. Mary Magdalene in the Old Fishmarket for a term of sixty years, at a yearly rent of xxxiij s. iiij d.*

On the 20th September, 23rd Hen. VIII. 1531, the Prioress and Convent leased two tenements, with two gardens adjoining to the same, within their close, to William Shelton, from the Michaelmas following, for twelve years, and, after the expiration of those years, for a term of fourscore and nineteen years, at a rent of 1 s. a year, payable at the four usual terms. The repairs were to be done by the farmer aforesaid.†

On the 26th January, 23rd Hen. VIII. 1531-2, they leased to Richard Berde aforesaid and Alice his wife a tenement in the parish of S. Ethelburga for a term of sixty years, at a yearly rent of xlv s. Repairs by the farmers.‡

On the 10th of June, 25th Henry VIII., 1533, Mary Rollesley, Prioress, and Convent entered into an agreement with Richard Berde aforesaid, citizen and girdler of London, by which, inasmuch as the late Prioress of S. Helen's, Dame Isabell Stampe, had, by a deed bearing date 1st Nov. in the 18th Hen. VIII. 1526, granted and let to Thomas Larke, citizen and Merchant Taylor, their great tenement or inn called the Black Bull, with cellars, &c., in the parish of S. Alburghe, in the Ward of Bishopsgate, and two adjoining tenements, for one and twenty years, from Midsummer following, at a yearly rent of 9l. 14s. sterling, they transferred the same to the said Richard at the same rent. If unpaid six weeks after due, the Prioress might enter and distrain. The agreement was allowed by the Court of Augmentations, on the 5th Jan., 32nd Hen. VIII., 1540-1.§

On the 10th of July, 25th Hen. VIII. 1533, they leased to the aforesaid William Shelton a tenement with appurtenances in their close, for a term of four score and eighteen years from the next following feast of the Nativity of S. John the Baptist, at a yearly rent of x s. payable at the four terms. Repairs by the farmer.‖

---

* Ministers' Accounts.   † Ibid.   ‡ Ibid.
§ Conventual Leases, No. 17. Orders and Decrees, vii, f. 35 b.
‖ Ministers' Accounts.

Among Dean Kentwode's orders, previously referred to, is the following regulation:

" Also for as moche that diúce fees ppetuell corrodies and lyuers have be grauntyd be for this tyme to diuerce officers of ȝowre house and other' psones whech have hurt the house and be cause of delapidacyoñ of the godys of ȝowre seyde house we ordeyne and jnioyne ȝow that ȝe reseyve noon officer' to noo ppetuell flee of office ne graunte noo annucte corody ne lyuery with out speciall assent of vs."

The examples subsequently given afford only too many instances of the violation of this good and prudent rule. The Prioress and Nuns of S. Helen's, however, were no exceptional case. The records of most Religious Houses present instances more or less numerous of the same exactions. That these were forced upon them by the unscrupulous we may be well assured, and that they endeavoured, although unsuccessfully, to abate the evil is no less indubitable.

On the 10th of September, 26th Hen. VIII., 1534, the Prioress and Convent gave to the infamous Thomas Crumwell, secretary of the king, an annuity of four marcs, issuing from their lands and tenements in London, for the term of his life, payable yearly at Michaelmas. If in arrear for three weeks, the said annuitant might enter and distrain. Four pence were paid immediately, as earnest and parcel of the annuity. This was allowed by the Court of Augmentations, with arrears from the dissolution of the House, on the 8th of February, 30th Hen. VIII. 1538-9.*

I hardly need tell the reader that this was one of those shameless extortions from which the Religious Houses were the sufferers during their last few years of tenure—offerings intended to propitiate a man of influence, who might subsequently be of assistance to the Community in the preservation of their rights. In the present instance the receiver was the implacable enemy of the victims that he pillaged, and a traitor alike to God and his

* Orders and Decrees, x. f. 131.

earthly sovereign. We shall subsequently meet, as I have said above, with several other grants of the same kind.

On the 10th September, 1534, they also leased to Richard Berde aforesaid a tenement in the parish of S. Alborough, in the ward of Bishopsgate, for a term of three score years, from Michaelmas next ensuing, at a yearly rent of xvjs. sterling, payable at two terms of the year. If in arrear for six weeks, the Prioress and Convent might enter and distrain.*

On the 1st of October, 26th Hen. VIII., 1534, Dame Mary Rollesley, Prioress, and Convent granted and leased to fee farm to John Rollesley, gent. all their manor of Burston or Bruston, in the county of Middlesex, with all the lands, tenements, woods, underwoods, court-leets, profits of courts, fines, amerciaments, and other profits and commodities whatsoever appertaining to the same manor, from the Michaelmas last past to the end of fourscore years next ensuing, at a yearly rent of 9l. payable at Lady Day and Michaelmas, in equal portions. Repairs were to be made by the aforesaid farmer. If the aforesaid rent or any parcel thereof were in arrear for forty days, the Prioress and Convent were to enter and distrain. This was allowed by the Court of Augmentations, on the 8th of November, 34 Hen. VIII. 1542.† The original of this lease still exists among the documents of the Augmentation Office, and has appended to it the common seal of the House, representing S. Helen, in agreement with the most important fact of her history, standing under the Cross which she embraces with her left arm, and holding in her left hand the three nails of the Passion. On the right, opposite to the empress, is a multitude of women with extended arms and upraised countenances. Beneath is a trefoiled niche, and under it a woman's (?) head and left arm in the same attitude as that of the figures above. The legend is SIGILL. MONIALIVM. SANCTE. HELENE. LONDONIARVM. Representations of this seal have been given by Malcolm and Wilkinson.‡

On the 2nd of December, 26th Hen. VIII. 1534, the Prioress

* Conventual Leases, No. 25.
† Ministers' Accounts. Orders and Decrees, xiii. f. 14 b.
‡ Malcolm, Lond. Rediv. iv. 548; Wilkinson, Lond. Illustr. i.

and Convent leased to Alan Hawte, his executors and assigns, a messuage with a garden within their close for a term of fourscore and nineteen years, at a yearly rent of 1 s. payable at Lady Day and Michaelmas in equal portions.   Repairs by the farmer.*

On the 24th December, 26th Hen. VIII., 1534, the Prioress and Convent appointed Sir James Bolleyne, knt., to be steward of their lands and tenements in London and elsewhere, the duties to be performed either by himself or a sufficient deputy, during the life of the said James, at a stipend of forty shillings a year, payable at Christmas.   If in arrear for six weeks, the said James might enter and distrain.   Allowed, with arrears from the Dissolution, by the Court of Augmentations, on the 10th of February, 30th Hen. VIII. 1538-9.†

On the 1st January, 26th Hen. VIII. 1534-5, Mary Rollesley, Prioress, and Convent made Richard Berde aforesaid, their seneschal, receiver and collector of all their manors, &c. by charter under the conventual seal, dated as aforesaid, for the term of his life from the date of the instrument, with a fee or stipend of 12l. sterling, and 20s. for his livery; also with eatables and drinkables, two cartloads of fuel and ten quarters of charcoal a-year allowed and delivered to him, and the use and occupation of one chamber, and of a certain parlour appertaining to the same, within the precinct of the Priory, with free ingress to and egress from the same at all convenient and lawful times during his life.‡

On the 20th of January, 1534-5, 26th Hen. VIII., the Prioress and Convent granted, demised, and let to Regnald or Rouland Goodman, citizen and fishmonger, their lands or great gardens, with a "Shedd" and other appurtenances, with free entry and issue, incoming and outgoing at all times convenient, requisite, and necessary, into and from the same, by and through the next way now used, had, and occupied, lying and being in the parish of S. Botolph without Bysshoppesgate, in the tenure of John Newton, " pulter," from Michaelmas, 1540, for fourscore years, at a yearly rent of four mares sterling, payable at Ladyday and Michaelmas, in equal por-

* Ministers' Accounts.
† Orders and Decrees, x. f. 141b.
‡ Conventual Leases, No. 20; Ministers' Accounts.

B

tions.   The said Rowland to keep and maintain competently all
the fences of the said lands or gardens.   If in arrear for a
quarter of a year, the Prioress and Convent to have again and
repossess their premises, as in their former estate.   Allowed by
the Court of Augmentations, on the 26th of November, 31st
Hen. VIII. 1539.*

On the 10th of December, 27th Hen. VIII. 1535, they
leased to John Rollesleye their messuage or mansion place, with
the gardens, cellars, solars, &c. appertaining to the same, lately
in the tenure of Nicholas late Bishop of Landaff, situated
between the tenements of Sir John Russell, knt. and Alen
Hawte, within the close of S. Helen's, from the Christmas following, for four score years, at a yearly rent of xlvjs. viijd.
sterling, payable at the four terms in even portions.   If in arrear
for thirteen weeks, the Prioress and Convent might enter and
distrain.   Repairs to be done by the farmer.   As in the other
instances given in the notes, the original lease still exists.†

On the 20th December, 27th Hen. VIII. 1535, they leased to
Thomas Pett, citizen and grocer, a messuage in the parish of
S. Ethelberga for a term of twenty years at a yearly rent of xlv s.‡

* Ministers' Accounts, Orders and Decrees, vi. f. 27.   Among the documents in the possession of the Leathersellers' Company is one of the same
year as the seven last described, 1534, and probably the counterpart of one
of them.   I regret that I cannot give positive information on this point, inasmuch as to my application to the Court of the Company for permission to
inspect it for a few minutes, in order to include its details in the present
memoir, that body thought fit to issue a refusal!   It is difficult to under-
stand the reason of such a repulse, further than that it appears to be a
sort of tradition with the Company to resist all such solicitations.   So
long ago as the year 1803 Malcolm complained that he "received no
encouragement in his inquiries."   "As it is," he adds, "what can be
viewed by the passenger I shall describe; but further this deponent
cannot say." (iii. 562.)   This jealous custody and concealment of documents,
which are now possessed simply of historical and archæological interest,
I had almost hoped were among the follies which have passed away—or,
at any rate, that it would not have found an apparently perpetual lodg-
ment in a worshipful Company of the City of London.

† Conventual Leases, No. 14.

‡ Ministers' Accounts.

On the 7th of April, in the 27th year of Hen. VIII., 1536, the Prioress and Convent granted, demised, and let to John Rolesley ten tenements, with gardens thereunto adjoining, and three chambers, with their appurtenances, situated within the close and tenements aforesaid; the tenements in the holding respectively of Richard Parker, Guy Crayford, Edward Waghan, Edward Bryseley, Margaret Dalton, widow, John Bernard, Richard Harman, John Harrocke, and Andrew Byscombe; and the chambers, one on the ground, in the tenure of Emma Lowe, widow, and the other two up the stairs, over the chambers of the said Emma, in the tenure of William Damerhawle; together with the alley, tenements, cellars, and solars, to the said alley appertaining, situated in the same close, (except a tenement or chamber in the said alley, wherein Johane Heyward then dwelt,) and another tenement outside the close, wherein Thomas Rancoke then dwelt, from Michaelmas last past for threescore years ensuing, at a yearly rent of £15, payable at the four usual terms of the year. The said John to keep the said premises in good and sufficient repair. If the rent were in arrear for six months after any of the said feasts, and no sufficient distress for the arrears could be found, the Prioress and Convent might re-enter and repossess. This was allowed by the Court of Augmentations, on the 17th of April, 31 Hen. VIII. 1540.*

On the same day the Prioress and Convent granted and let to the same John their tenements with appurtenances in the parish of S. Alphe in "Muggewell Strete," and S. Olave in "Silver Strete by Crepulgate," from Michaelmas next coming for a term of fourscore years, at a yearly rent of £7 sterling, payable at the usual terms. The said John to keep the premises in competent and sufficient repair. If the rent were in arrear for six weeks, the Prioress and Convent were to have power to enter and distrain. If for a quarter of a year, or if the repairs were not accomplished in avoiding rain and other extreme weather, they might re-enter and repossess themselves wholly of the property.

* Conventual Leases, No. 15. Ministers' Accounts. Orders and Decrees, v. f. 1.

This was allowed by the Court of Augmentations on the 20th April, 31 Hen. VIII. 1540.*

On the same day, the Prioress and Convent leased to John Rollesleye, his executors and assigns, two tenements in the parish of S. Elen outside the close, one in the tenure of William Shurburne, citizen and barber-surgeon, and a marsh called the " Hare Marsshe " in the parish of Stebunheth in the county of Middlesex, for a term of sixty years, at a rent of viij li. xvs. iiijd. payable at the four usual terms.†

In the 27th of Hen. VIII. the " Valor" was taken of all ecclesiastical property, to determine the tenth which was henceforth ordered to be paid to the King for the support of his new-fledged dignity of Supreme Head of the Church of England. The yearly value of all the possessions of the House was £376 6s., in rents from tenements in the city of London, the rectory of S. Helen, tenements in Bordeston and Edelmeton in Middlesex, Eyworth in Bedfordshire, Barmeling in Kent, Balamesmede and Marck in Essex, Ware in Hertford, and Dachet in Buckingham. Out of this sum various rents for lands in several parishes of the city were to be deducted, together with the stipends of Sir James Bulleyn, knight, chief steward, Richard Berde, receiver, and John Dodington, auditor; and pensions to David Netley, chaplain of the perpetual chantry of the B. V. M. in the Church of S. Helen; Thomas Criche, chaplain of the chantry of the Holy Ghost, in the same church; the churchwardens of S. Mary Botowe; the wardens of a fraternity in Bow Church; Thomas More, chaplain of a chantry in S. Michael's, Cornhill; poor people at the anniversaries of Adam Fraunces, Robert Knolls, and Hugh Wynarde, in the Church of S. Helen; the vicar of Eyworth ; the Bishop of Lincoln, for sinodals and procurations; and the Abbess and Convent of Barking. These amounted to £55 10s. 3½d., leaving clear £320 15s. 8½d.; the tenth to be deducted from which was £32 1s. 7d.‡

On the 6th October, 28th Hen. VIII. 1536, they leased to

---

* Ministers' Accounts.   Orders and Decrees, v. f. 2.

† Conventual Leases, No. 9.   Ministers' Accounts.

‡ Val. Eccl. v. i. pp. 392, 393.

John Dodington a tenement called "the Sterre" at Ware, with all its chambers, cellars, solars, &c. for a term of sixty years from the next following Michaelmas, at a yearly rent of xl s. payable at Lady Day and Michaelmas, in equal portions. Repairs to be done by the aforesaid farmer.*

On the 20th of May, 29th Hen. VIII. 1537, the Prioress and Convent granted to Richard Wolverston, yeoman, for sundry good services, an annuity of twenty shillings sterling, issuing as before, for the term of his life, payable in equal portions at Christmas and Midsummer. If in arrear for six weeks, the said Richard might enter and distrain. Allowed, with arrears from the Dissolution, by the Court of Augmentations, on the 12th of February, 30th Hen. VIII. 1538-9.†

On the 30th May, 29th Hen. VIII. 1537, they leased to John Thurgood, his executors and assigns, a tenement with shops, cellars, solars, &c. in Ivelane, in the parish of S. Faith in Paternoster Rowe, for a term of fifty-one years from the Lady Day of that year, at a yearly rent of liij s. iiij d. payable at the four usual terms. Repairs by the farmer.‡

On the 1st July, 29th Hen. VIII. 1537, they leased to Richard Stafferton a tenement, with shops, cellars, solars, &c. in the parish of S. Mary Wolnoth, for a term of fifty years, at a yearly rent of xxiij s. iiij d. payable at the four terms.§

On the 1st of December, 29 Henry VIII. 1537, they leased to Sir Arthur Darcy, knt. a messuage within their close, late in the occupation of Thomas Benolt the herald, from Michaelmas last past, for a term of four score and sixteen years, at a rent of xls., payable at the four usual terms. Repairs by the farmer.‖

On the 1st December, 29th(?) Hen. VIII. 1537, the Prioress and Convent granted to John Dodington an annuity of xl s. for the term of his life, payable in equal portions at Easter and Michaelmas.¶

On the 2nd of December, 29 Henry VIII. 1537, they leased to

* Conventual Leases, No. 18.   Ministers' Accounts.
† Orders and Decrees, x. f. 164 b.
‡ Ministers' Accounts.   § Ibid.
‖ Conventual Leases, No. 11.   ¶ Ministers' Accounts.

Elizabeth Hawte, widow, their tenement or messuage, with cellars, solars, gardens, woodhouses, stables, &c. " abbutting vpon the well yarde in the said l⁹orye on the westt, one other parte therof ending at the gate called the tymber halle gate buttyng vpon the Inner dorter on the East pte, the other pte therof w^t the gardeyne therto adioynyng stretching alonge the ffrater on the sowthe parte, and the other parte therof lyeng alonge the cartewaye goyng into the tymber yarde on the north parte," from the Christmas following for fifty years, at a yearly rent of xxs. sterling, payable at the four terms.   The Prioress and Convent to keep in repair.*

On the 20th of December, 29th Hen. VIII., 1537, the Prioress and Convent granted to John Dodyngton, gent. aforesaid, auditor of their accounts, to have the first advowson, nomination, and presentation of their vicarage of Eyworth, in the county of Bedford and diocese of Lincoln, for one single turn, whenever the said vicarage should by death, resignation, promotion, or in any other way, chance to be vacant, as fully and entirely as they themselves the patrons. Allowed by the Court of Augmentations on the 9th of February, 35th Hen. VIII. 1543–4.†

On the 21st of January, 29th Henry VIII. 1537–8, the Prioress and Convent granted to John Sewstre, gent., for good counsel, past and future, an annual pension of four mares, issuing as before, for the term of his life, in equal portions at Lady Day and Michaelmas. If in arrear for five weeks, the said John to have power to enter and distrain. Allowed, with arrears, by the Court of Augmentations on the 12th February, 30th Hen. VIII. 1538–9.‡

On the 16th March, 29th Henry VIII. 1537–8, they leased to Nicholas De la Mare, priest, one little tenement on the north side of the close or churchyard, from Lady Day following, for the term of the ensuing forty years, at a yearly rent of xs. payable at Michaelmas and Lady Day. If in arrear for half a year, the

---

* Conventual Leases, No. 16.
† Orders and Decrees, xiv. f. 78.
‡ Ministers' Acounts. Orders and Decrees, x. f. 149.

Prioress and Convent might enter and distrain. The lessors were to do all necessary repairs. If the said Nicholas died before the end of the aforesaid term, a month after his decease the lease to be void, and of no effect.*

On the same 16th of March, 29th Hen. VIII. 1537-8, they leased a tenement to David Necton, for a term of forty years from the following Lady Day, at a yearly rent of x s., payable at Lady Day and Michaelmas in equal portions.†

On the 20th March, 1537–8, they granted to Thomas Pereye, citizen and skinner, the renewal of a lease, which Alice Tracthall, a former Prioress, had granted to Thomas Knyght, by indenture dated the 20th March, 13th Henry VII. 1497–8, of a tenement or "brue hous called the Scomer vpon the Hope, sett and being in Byrchin Lane, and a plour sett on the northe syde of the halle dore of the said tent Bruchous towarde the Strete," &c. from Lady Day, 1547, when that lease would expire, to the end of a term of three score years, at a yearly rent of vj li. xiij s. iiij d. sterling, payable at the four terms. If in arrear for six weeks, the Prioress and Convent to enter and distrain; if for fourteen weeks, to repossess. Repairs by the farmer. The lessors or their deputies might examine the premises twice in every year, to see that the farmer fulfilled his engagement.‡

On the 28th of March, 29th Hen. VIII. 1538, they leased to Antony Bonvixi, merchant, their great messuage, with all houses, solars, cellars, gardens, &c. called Crosbyes Place, together with nine messuages belonging to the same, for a term of seventy-one years, immediately after the end and completion of a term of ninety-nine years to John Crosbye, citizen and grocer of London, viz. from the feast of the Nativity of S. John the Baptist, 1565, at a yearly rent of xj li. vj s. viij d. payable at the usual terms.§

On the 30th of March, 29th Hen. VIII., 1538, the Prioress

* Conventual Leases, No. 12.
† Ministers' Accounts.
‡ Conventual Leases, No. 6.
§ Conventual Leases, No. 10. Part. for grants, Antony Bonvyxe. Ministers' Accounts.

and Convent granted to Edward Rollesley, gent., in consideration of good and faithful service, an annuity of forty shillings sterling, issuing as before, for the term of his life, payable at Lady Day and Michaelmas in equal portions. If in arrear, the said Edward might enter and distrain. The said Edward was put into possession by a payment to him of fourpence. Allowed by the Court of Augmentations, with arrears from the Dissolution, on the 26th of October, 31st Hen. VIII. 1539.*

On the 12th April, 29th Henry VIII. 1538, they leased to Robert Owterede, citizen and cordwainer, two tenements outside the close, for a term of thirty years, at a rent of xlvj s. viij d. payable at the usual terms.†

On the 17th April, 1538, they renewed to Domenic Lomelyn a lease formerly made to him by Isabell Stampe, Prioress of S. Helen's, dated the 3rd of December, 4th Henry VIII. 1512, of a tenement in S. Elen's, for four score and eleven years, at a yearly rent of x li. x s. sterling. If in arrear for six weeks, the Prioress and Convent to enter and distrain.‡

On the 20th June, 30th Hen. VIII. 1538, they leased to John Melshame a tenement in Chepesyde, in the parish of S. Matthew in Ffrydaye Strete, with shops, solars, cellars, &c., " wherof one shoppe hath the signe of the Mylke mayde w* tankarde on her hedde, and the other shoppe hath the signe of the Cowe," from the Midsummer following, for a term of forty years, at a yearly rent of vj li. xiij s. iiij d. payable at the four usual terms.§

On the 26th June, 30th Hen. VIII., 1538, the Prioress and Convent granted to John Rollesley, gent., for good counsel past and future, an annuity of four marcs sterling, issuing as before, for the term of his life, payable in equal portions, at Ladyday and Michaelmas. If in arrear for one month, the said John might enter and distrain. Allowed, with arrears from the Dissolution, by the Court of Augmentations, on the 24th of April, 31st Hen. VIII. 1539.‖

* Orders and Decrees, vi. f. 47b.   † Ministers' Accounts.
‡ Conventual Leases, No. 26.
§ Conventual Leases, No. 8. Ministers' Accounts.
‖ Orders and Decrees, x. f. 298b.

On the 30th June, 30th Hen. VIII. 1538, Mary, the Prioress, and Convent gave to Henry Bowsell, gentleman, of London, a certain annuity or annual rent of ten shillings, issuing from their lands and tenements in the city of London. It was granted in reward of good counsel given previously, and to be rendered in time to come, and was to be paid in equal portions at Christmas and Midsummer. If it were unpaid for the time of six weeks, the said Henry might enter and distrain. This was allowed by the Court of Augmentations on the 28th January, 34th Hen. VIII. 1542–3.*

On the same day the Prioress and Convent granted to Henry Bowsfell, gent., for good counsel, &c., and certain other considerations then moving them, a certain annuity or annual rent of twenty-six shillings and eightpence sterling, issuing from their property in London and elsewhere, for the term of his life, payable yearly at Christmas and Midsummer, in equal portions. If in arrear, in part or in whole, for six weeks, the aforesaid Henry might enter and distrain. Allowed, with arrears from the Dissolution, by the Court of Augmentations, on the 17th of October, 31st Hen. VIII. 1539.†

On the 1st July, 30th Hen. VIII. 1538, they leased to William Shyrborne a tenement with cellars, solars, &c. outside the close, from the feast of the Nativity of S. John the Baptist in that year, for a term of thirty years, at a yearly rent of xx s. payable at the usual terms.‡

On the 2nd July, 30th Henry VIII. 1538, they leased to William Shelton two tenements in the parish of S. Mary at Naxe, for a term of fourscore years from the following Michaelmas, at a yearly rent of xls. payable at the four terms. If in arrear for a quarter of a year, the Prioress and Convent might enter and distrain. Repairs by the farmer.§

On the 9th July, 30th Henry VIII. 1538, the Prioress and Convent granted to Jerome Shelton, gent., for good counsel past and future, an annuity or annual rent of four marcs sterling,

* Orders and Decrees, xiii. f. 126 b.   † Ibid. vi. f. 114 b.
‡ Ministers' Accounts.
§ Conventual Leases, No. 7.   Ministers' Accounts.

C

issuing from their tenements in the city of London or elsewhere, for the term of his life, payable at Christmas and Midsummer, in equal portions. If in arrear for forty days, the said Jerome might enter and distrain. The Court of Augmentations continued this payment to the said Jerome, with arrears from the Dissolution of the House, on the 12th of February, 30 Hen. VIII. 1538-9.[*]

On the same day, the Prioress and Convent granted to Roger Hall, for good and faithful service, an annuity of twenty shillings, issuing as before, for the term of his life, payable at Christmas and Midsummer. If in arrear for five weeks, the said Roger might enter and distrain. Allowed, with arrears from the Dissolution, by the Court of Augmentations, on' the 19th of November, 32nd Hen. VIII. 1540.[†]

On the same day, the Prioress and Convent granted to John Staverton, gent., for good counsel, &c., an annuity of four marcs sterling, issuing as before, for the term of his life, payable at Christmas and Midsummer, in equal portions. If in arrear for fourteen days, the said John might enter and distrain. Allowed, with arrears from the Dissolution, by the Court of Augmentations, on the 20th November, 32nd Hen. VIII. 1540[‡]

On the 1st August, 30th Henry VIII. 1538, they leased to John Rollesley their manor of Marke, with all and singular its appurtenances, situated in the parishes of Leyton and Walcombestowe, in the county of Essex, together with all its lands, tenements, rents, services, &c. for a term of fourscore years from the next following Michaelmas, at a yearly rent of viij li. payable at Lady Day and Michaelmas in equal portions. Repairs to be done by the aforesaid farmer.[§]

On the 20th August, 30th Henry VIII. 1538, they leased to Thomas Persey one messuage with shops, cellars, solars, &c. in the parish of S. Martin Owtewiche, for a term of sixty years, at a yearly rent of liij s iiij d. payable at the four usual terms.[‖]

---

* Orders and Decrees, x. f. 127.   † Ibid. viii. f. 56 b.
‡ Ibid. viii. f. 89 b.
§ Conventual Leases, No. 21. Ministers' Accounts.
‖ Ministers' Accounts.

On the 1st September, 30th Henry VIII. 1538, they leased to
Richard Staverton a messuage with appurtenances in the parish
of S. Mary Magdalene in the Old Fishmarket, for a term of
fourscore years, at a yearly rent of lxvj s. viij d.*

On the 10th of September, 30th Henry VIII. 1538, they
leased to Richard Staverton aforesaid, his executors and assigns,
two tenements outside the close for a term of fourscore years
from the Michaelmas of the same year, at a rent of xlvj s. viij d.
payable at the usual terms.†

On the same day they leased to Richard Staverton aforesaid a
tenement in the parish of S. Matthew in ffrydayestrete, for a term
of fourscore years, at a yearly rent of lxvj s. viij d. payable at the
four usual terms.‡

On the same day they leased to the aforesaid Richard Staverton, his executors and assigns, two tenements in the parish of S.
John in Walbrooke, for a term of fourscore years, at a rent of
lxxvj s. viij d. payable at the four terms.§

On the 1st of October, 30th Hen. VIII. 1538, the Prioress and
Convent granted to John Melsham, gent., for good counsel, &c.,
an annuity of twenty shillings, issuing as before, for the term of
his life, payable at Lady Day and Michaelmas, in equal portions.
If in arrear for five weeks, the aforesaid John might enter and
distrain. Allowed by the Court of Augmentations on the 22nd
November, 32nd Hen. VIII. 1540.‖

On the 4th of October, 30th Henry VIII. 1538, they leased to
Antony Bonvixi, his executors and assigns, a tenement with
solars, cellars, &c. situated in a certain alley within their close,
over the "larder-house" and the "cole-house" of the said Antony, and lately in the tenure of Julian Fraunces, for a term of
fourscore years from the feast of Michaelmas in that year, at a
yearly rent of x s. payable at the usual terms. Repairs were
to be made by the farmer.¶

* Ministers' Accounts.
† Ibid.　　　　　　　　‡ Ibid.　　　　　　　§ Ibid.
‖ Orders and Decrees, viii. f. 81.
¶ Conventual Leases, No. 22. Part. for grants, Antony Bonvyxe, and
Ministers' Accounts.

This was the last act of the Prioress and Convent before the event which removed from them the power of entering into any similar engagements for the time to come. In less than two months afterwards the storm had fallen upon them, and all was over. The unhappy Sisters, like hundreds of others in similar establishments, were ruthlessly expelled from their ancient home, to encounter the dangers of a world of which they had hitherto little or no experience. The original deed of Surrender still exists in the Record Office. There are no signatures to this document, which was forced on the sufferers against their will, already prepared before it was submitted to their acceptance, and slightly concealing, under a flimsy disguise of law, an act of the basest and most shameless despotism. The common seal of the Priory was appended; but only a fragment of it now remains. The document bears date the 25th of November, 30th Hen. VIII., 1538—not 1539, as the editors of Dugdale have stated in error.

The names of the last Prioress and Sisters, so far as I can recover them, were Mary Rollesley, Prioress, and Margaret Sampson, Elizabeth Graye, Katherine Glassappe, Joan Pamplyn, Elionor Hanham, and Ann Aleyne, Sisters. The latter were surviving in 1556. It is probable that half were by that time dead. But we have no certain account of the number who witnessed the destruction of their House, or of the dreadful interval. Those were days of silent and secret martyrdom, inflicted on victims least able to endure the terrible ordeal.

It is not unlikely that the last named Sister was daughter of the John Aleyn and Agnes his wife to whom the Prioress and Convent, on the 19th of July, 12th Henry VIII., 1520, leased a tenement in the parish of S. Olave by London Bridge, called the "Sonne," alias the "Salutacyon," and a messuage adjacent to the same, for the term of the life of the survivor, at a yearly rent of six pounds thirteen shillings and four pence.* Was she related also to the famous Bishopsgate benefactor, the munificent Edward Alleyne, born in the parish of S. Botolph, on the 1st of September, 1566, and founder of Dulwich College in 1619?

* Ministers' Accounts.

Roger Hall, already mentioned, was janitor of the west-gate of the close, and with Alice his wife was at the Dissolution of the Priory in possession of a house worth 10 s. a year.* At the time of the Suppression the Prioress received a gratuity of xxx li. and the grant of an annual pension of x li ;† and four annuities, or "perpetual pensions," in behalf of the dissolved House, amounting yearly to the sum of cxij s. ij d. ob. were paid by the Government to "the Deane and Chapiter of Pawles" in the 34th, 35th, 36th, 37th, and 38th years of Hen. VIII.‡

In the year 1556 the annuities and pensions paid to the former officers and inmates of the Priory were as follow:

S. HELEN'S LATE PRIORY.

Annuities.

Edward Rowlesley	. . xl s.	
John Rowlesley	. . . liij s.	iiij d.
Richard Berde	. . . xl s.	
John Melsham	. . . xx s.	

Pensions.

Margaret Sampson.	. . liij s.	iiij d.
Elizabeth Graye	. . . liij s.	iiij d.
Katherine Glassappe	. . liij s.	iiij d.
Joan Pamplyn	. . . lxvj s.	viij d.
Elionor Hanham	. . . liij s.	iiij d.
Ann Aleyne .	. . . liij s.	iiij d.§

This is the last mention which I find of the Sisters in any of the records of the period.

We have already seen that there were two Chantries in the church of S. Helen, the priests of which received annual stipends from the Priory. These incumbents at the time of the "Valor," in 1536, were

David Netley, B. V. M.	. viij li.
Thomas Criche, Holy Ghost	vij li.

* Ministers' Accounts.
† Misc. Books, Off. Aug. vol. 245, n. 228.
‡ Misc. Books, Off. Aug. vols. 248, 249, 250, 256, 262.
§ Cardinal Pole's Pension Book, f. iii.

In the Ministers' Accounts, 31-32 Hen. VIII. we find
Nicholas de la Mer, B. V. M. founded for
   the soul of Adam Fraunces   . .   viij li.
Thomas Ryson, Holy Ghost, founded for
   the soul of Adam Fraunces,   . .   vij li.
Thomas Wynestanley, Nuns' chaplain   vj li. xiij s. iiij d.

In the Certificate of Chantries and Fraternities, 2nd Edward
VI. the names of the last incumbents are thus given, with their
previous stipends and post-Dissolution pensions:

S. Ellens.

Thomas Wynston, vj li. xiij s. iiij d.   pension c s.
Thomas Robson   vij li. . . .   ,,   c s.

In the Particulars for the Sale of the Chantry Lands we learn
that certain property in S. Helen's of this nature was sold on the
24th December, 3 Edward VI. 1549, and on the 26th January,
3 Edward VI. 1549-50, to John Roulande, page of the King's
wardrobe, and was " past in the names of John Dodington and
William Warde, as parcel of the sum of Mcclxxv li. iiij s. viij d."[*]

Lastly, from Cardinal Pole's Pension Book we learn that the
priests before mentioned were still living in 1556.

CHANTRIES IN THE CHURCH OF S. HELEN.

Pensions.

Thomas Robson, lately incumbent there .   c s.
Thomas Wynstanley, lately incumbent there   c s.[†]

Of the scene of these transactions, much less than could be
desired is now to be known. Not a stone remains to tell of
the House and its glories. A view of the place as it existed
at the close of the last century, which is happily furnished by
Wilkinson in his *Londina*, represents the ruins of edifices whose
main portions and features are of the Early English period, and
which were probably coeval with the foundation of the Priory.
These he calls the " Remains of the Fratry." He had the advan-

* Parts. for Sale of Chantries, vol. i. p. 270 b.
† Cardinal Pole's Pension Book, f. iiii.

PART OF THE PRIORY OF S. HELEN, BISHOPSGATE, DESTROYED IN 1799.

[From an original drawing in the possession of J. E. Gardner, Esq.]

tage of a personal examination of these beautiful memorials. "The door," he says, "leading from the cloister to the fratry, which the writer of this well remembers to have seen at the late demolition of it, was particularly elegant, the mouldings of the upper part being filled with roses of stone painted scarlet and gilt; the windows of the fratry itself also, which were nearly lancet-shaped, were extremely beautiful." He also gives two views of the beautiful "crypt," and one of the hall above it; the former of which is in the Early-English style, while the latter has ornamental additions of post-Dissolution times. It appears by his plan that there were at least two "crypts," one under the hall, and another to the south, under what would be called the withdrawing room. It is the former which is represented in his engravings. Of the latter I am glad that the kindness of a friend* has enabled me to present the reader with an original and most interesting delineation (*see the engraving*). The part represented—the eastern end of the southern "crypt"—may easily be identified by an inspection of Wilkinson's plan. This was evidently of the same style as that which adjoined it, the beautiful Early-English. My second illustration, which is of no less interest and value, is taken from an original drawing in the British Museum (*see the engraving*), which I am permitted to copy by favour of the Trustees.

Of contemporary descriptions, that contained in the "Valor" simply makes mention of the "seite of the Priory, with the court-yards and little gardens, with divers houses situated within the precinct." And the Ministers' Accounts are similarly meagre. A few particulars, already given from several of the leases, necessarily refer to the adjoining premises rather than to the Priory itself. Stowe, Howel, and others furnish us with nothing to supply the deficiency. Truly valuable, therefore, and by far the most interesting description of the House with which I am acquainted, is the following Survey of the King's Officers, pre-

* I have much pleasure in offering my thanks for this favour to John E. Gardner, Esq. whose collection of original drawings and engravings of London localities is only equalled by his kindness and courtesy in placing his stores at the disposal of his friends.

liminary to the disposal of the property. It is a picture of the
place as the Nuns left it, and before the changes which soon
afterwards ensued:

"The late Priorye of Saint Elenes within the Citye of London.
The View and Surveye ther taken the xxi[th] daye of June, in
the xxxiij Yeare of the raigne of our Soveraigne Lord Kinge
Henrye the viij[th], by Thomas Mildmay, one of the King's Audi-
tors thereunto assigned. That is to saye,

"The Parisshe of Saint Elenes, within the Citie of London.
The Scite of the late Priory their.

"Fyrste, the cheaf entre or cominge in to the same late Priory
ys in and by the street gate lyying in the pishe of S[t] Elenes,
in Bysshopsgate Streat, which leadeth to a little cowrte next
adioyning to the same gate, havinge chambers, howses, and buyl-
dinges, environinge the same, out of w[ch] cowrte there is an entre
leadinge to an inner cowrte, w[ch] on the North side is also like-
wise environed wth edificyons and buyldings, called the Stewardes
lodging, with a Countinge house apperteninge to the same. Item,
next to the same cowrte ther ys a faire Kechinge, withe a pastery
house, larder houses, and other howses of office, apperteninge to
the same; and at the Est ende of the same Kechyn and entre
leadinge to the same hall, wth a litle plor adioyning, having
under the same hall and plor sondrie howses of office, next
adioyning to the Cloyster ther, and one howse called the Covent
plor. Item, iij fair Chambers adioyninge to the hall, whearof
the one over the entree leadinge to the cloyster, thother over the
Buttree, and the third over the larder. Item, from the said
entre by the hall, to the Cloyster, w[ch] cloyster yet remaneth
holly leaded, and at the North side of the same cloyster a fare
long howse called the Fratree. Item, at thest end of the same
Cloyster, a lodginge called the Suppryors lodging, wth a litle
gardin lieng to the same. And by the same lodginge a pare of
staires leading to the Dortor, at the Scuthend whearof ther is a
litle hows, wherein the Evidence of the said hows nowe dou
remayne, wth all howses and lodginges vnder the same Dorter.
Item, at the Westende of the same cloyster, a dore leadinge in
to the nunes late Quire, extending from the dore out of the

churche yarde unto the lampe or pticyon deviding the priorye from the pisshe, wch is holly leaded. Item, at thest ende of the said cloyster, an entre leading to a little Garden, and out of the same littell garden to a faire garden called the Covent Garden, côteninge by estimaçn half an acre. And, at the Northend of the said garden, a dore leading to another garden called the Kechin garden; and at the Westende of the same ther is a Dovehowsshe; and in the same garden a dore to a faire Woodyerd, wth howses, pticons, and gardens, w^{th}in the same Woodyerd a tenement, wth a garden, a stable, and other thapptances to the same belonginge, called Elizabeth Hawtes lodginge. All which p̃misses ben rated, extentyd, and valued, The Kings highnesse to be discharged of the repaçons, of the yerely value of

vj li. xiij s. iiij d.

" Item, one Tenement their in, in the hold of Wittm. Baker, by the yeare,   xx s.

" Item, one ʼother Tenement, in the hold of Jane Julian, by the yeare,   xiij s. iiij d.

" Item, one other Tenement ther, in the hold of Edmûde Brewer, by the yeare,   xiij s. iij d.

" Item, one other Tenement ther, in the hold of Gye Sturdye, by the yeare,   xiij s. iiij d.

" Item, one other Tenement ther, in the hold of Lanclott Harryson, by the yeare,   xiij s. iiij d.

viij li. xiij s. iiij d.

Sm^{a} x li. vj s. viij. d.

Ex^{m} p me THOMAM MILDMAIE, Auditor'."[*]

It will be interesting to compare this description with the bird's-eye view of the place in Aggas's Map of London, 1560. The resemblance, although not striking, is nevertheless perceptible. (See the engraving on the next page.)

The House was evidently a large and goodly collection of edifices. You entered from Bishopsgate Street by a gateway into a court surrounded by the more humble buildings of the Community, and from thence into an inner court which con-

* Archæol. xvi. 29. Malcolm, Lond. Red. iii. 550, 551.

D

tained some of the more important offices, the steward's lodging
and counting-house, the kitchen, pastry-house, larder, and other
apartments, the entrance to the hall and an adjoining parlour,
with offices below them, as well as that to the cloister and the
Convent parlour. The entrance to the cloister, the buttery, and

Bishopp gate Strate   *S. Elen*   *Papye*   *S. Mare axe*

larder had each an elegant chamber above them adjoining the
hall. Next came the Cloister, on the north of which was a long
and goodly building, called the Fratry, and on the east the
lodging of the Sub-prioress with its garden. Adjoining this a
flight of stairs led to the dormitory, south of which was a small
house, in which were deposited the various leases and other legal
documents connected with the conventual property. West of the
cloister a door led to the Nuns' church. An entry on the east
side, by the Sub-prioress's lodging and the dormitory, introduced
you to a little garden, and thence to the fair pleasure-garden of
the House. At the north end of this a door led to the kitchen
garden, with a dove-house at its western end; and a further door
communicated with a capacious wood yard, which embraced
various inclosures, tenements, gardens, a stable, and other appurtenances. Such was the home of the Nuns of S. Helen's.

The north aisle of the Church of S. Helen was "the Nunnes Quire," and was divided, by a screen from pier to pier of the arcade, from the part appropriated to the parish. One of the fastenings, or a piece of iron popularly considered so to be, is still to be seen occupying its original position on the east side of one of the piers. In the wall of this aisle is a curious hagioscope, which at first sight looks like an altar-tomb. Its base is ornamented with panels, and through these, which although now filled up behind were pierced with oblique openings, an altar at the east end of the same aisle might have been seen from the so-called "crypt," which, I believe, was used by the Nuns as a cloister. There is a view of it in Malcolm, and one of a somewhat similar design, at Chipping Norton, is figured in the Glossary of Architecture, plate 194. In the same wall a doorway remains, bricked up and indeed half buried, by which the Sisters obtained access from the Cloister to the Church. The level of the sill is about three feet below the present pavement.

I have, lastly, to furnish the reader with some account of the dispersion of the spoil, so far as regards the site of the house, and of the various adjoining tenements in and about the close.

On the 21st of April, 30th Henry VIII. 1539, the King granted to Balthazar Gwercy, of the city of London, surgeon, and Joan his wife, certain tenements, gardens, &c in the parishes of S. Mary at Nax and S. Andrew Undershafte in consideration of £71 10s. the property to be held of the King in chief by the service of a twentieth part of one knight's fee, and a yearly rent of xxvj s. viij d. payable at Michaelmas.*

On the 3rd of October, 31st Henry VIII. 1539, the King granted to Guy Crafford, Esq. and Joan his wife, in consideration of the sum of £54, a messuage or tenement, with cellars, solars, stables, gardens, &c. situated in the parish of S. Helen, and within the close of the late Priory, formerly in the tenure of Thomas Benolt, then in that of Sir Arthur Darcy, knt. and lastly in that of the aforesaid Guy. Also another messuage adjoining the same on the west, and lately in the tenure of

* Ministers' Accounts. Pat. 30 Hen. VIII. p. 8, mm. 8 (20), 7 (21).

George Taylour, gent. Both were among the possessions of the
late Priory, and were to be held from Lady Day last past by the
service of a twentieth part of one knight's fee, and a yearly rent
of six shillings and eight pence by name of tithe payable at
Michaelmas. The grant was made without fine great or small,
and was dated, witness the King at Westminster, on the day
aforesaid.*

On the 3rd of March, 31st Henry VIII., 1539-40, the King
granted to William Crane, Esq. and Margaret his wife, and their
heirs, ten tenements, within the close and circuit of the late
Priory of S. Helen, then in the tenure of John Parker, Guy
Crayford, Hugh Vaughan, Edward Brysseley, Margaret Dalton,
John Barnard, Richard Herman, John Harrope, and Adrian
Byscombe; three chambers, in the tenure of William Damarall and
Emma Lawe, within the close; and six chambers in the tenure
of Richard Atkyns, Alice Paule, Reginald Deane, Elizabeth
Watson, and the aforesaid William, situated in a certain alley
within the close; a tenement in the tenure of John Parker
within the close, in the parish of S. Andrew Undershaft; and
another tenement in the tenure of the said William within the
close, all belonging to the said late Priory, and leased to John
Rollesley. The property was to be held by the service of a
twentieth part of one knight's fee, and a yearly rent of thirty-
four shillings and eightpence. The grant is dated at Westminster, on the day above mentioned.†

Then came the grant of the site of the House itself.

On the 29th of March, 33rd Hen. VIII., 1542, the King
granted to Sir Richard Williams, knt., alias Crumwell, in ex-
change for the manors of Brampton and Hemyngford Grey,
in the county of Huntingdon, and for the sum of £731 0s. 7½d.
sterling, various lands in the counties of Glamorgan, Herts,
Huntingdon, Bedford, Norfolk, &c. Also the whole of the
site, sept, circuit, and precinct of the late Priory of S. Helen,
the church vulgarly called " the Nonnes Churche of Seynt

* Pat. 31 Hen. VIII. p. 4, m. (35) 20. Orig. 31st Hen. VIII. p. 1, r. lv.
† Pat. 31 Hen. VIII. p. 7, m. 1 (32). Orig. 31st Hen. VIII. p. 2, r. ccv.

Helyns," and all and singular messuages, houses, buildings, &c., &c., belonging to the said site. Also certain messuages in the tenure or occupation of William Baker, Jane Julyan, Edmund Brewer, Guy Sturdye, and Lancelot Harrison, or their assigns. Added to this horrible amount of sacrilege, other lands in the counties of Devon, Herts, Huntingdon, and others, lately belonging to the dissolved monasteries of Ramsey, Nethe, S. Alban's, Huntingdon, Forde, Yermouth, &c. The property was to be held in chief, by the service of a tenth part of one knight's fee and the payment of various yearly rents for the different portions, that for the S. Helen's property amounting to thirty-nine shillings and ninepence farthing sterling, for all services and demands. The grant bears date, witness the King, at Westminster, on the day above mentioned.*

On the 9th September, 34th Henry VIII. 1542, the King granted to Antony Bonvixi, merchant, in return for the sum of £207 18s. 4d. together with certain property in Essex, the reversion of Crosbyes Place, and all solars, cellars, gardens, lanes, messuages, tenements, void pieces of ground, and all other appurtenances thereunto belonging. It had been already leased to him, as we have seen, by indenture dated 28th March, 29th Hen. VIII. 1538. Also various curtilages in the parish of S. Mary at Naxe, leased to the same on the 4th October, 30th Hen. VIII., 1538. Crosbyes Place with appurtenances was valued at the clear yearly sum of £11 16s. 8d. and the property in the adjoining parish at that of 12s. The former was to be held in chief, by the service of a fortieth part of one knight's fee and the payment of a yearly rent of twenty-three shillings and eight pence of lawful money of England payable at Michaelmas by name of tithe. The latter also in chief, by the service of a hundredth part of one knight's fee, and a similar rent of 15d. payable at Michaelmas. The grant was dated, witness the King, at Westminster, the 9th December, 1542.†

* Pat. 33 Hen. VIII. p. 6, mm. 37 (16)—34 (19). Orig. 33rd Hen. VIII. p. 3, r. xxi.
† Pat. 34 Hen. VIII. p. 1, mm. 14 (13)—12 (15). Orig. 34th Hen. VIII. p. 1, r. xvi.

On the 16th July, 35th Hen., VIII. 1543, the King granted to
Roland Goodman, citizen of London, for £146 0s. 6d., the property formerly leased to him, a tenement called "le Shedd,"
lately in the tenure of John Newton, with a garden and three closes
of land, in the parish of S. Botolph without Bishopsgate, and
belonging to the Priory. Property belonging to other houses
accompanied the aforesaid. That of S. Helen's was to be held in
chief by the service of a hundredth part of one knight's fee and
a yearly rent of five shillings and four pence. The grant was
dated, witness the King, at Terling, on the day before named.*
The original instrument is still preserved among the Harleian
Charters, a large sheet of parchment, with a pen and ink minia-
ture of the royal dealer in the upper left-hand corner, and a
tolerable impression of the Great Seal appendant at the foot.†

On the 24th September, 36th Henry VIII. 1544, the King
granted to Roger Higham and William Grene, among other possessions of various London houses, divers tenements in the parish
of S. Helen lately in the tenure of William Shirborne, Robert
Owtred, William Plumpton, Richard Kyrton, William Hunte
" wever," John Dymmocke, and Richard Staverton, with other
tenements in the parish of S. Ethelburga and elsewhere, belonging to the late Priory. The annual value of these amounted to
the sum of £19 12s. 8d. and they were to be held in free bur-
gage for all services and demands. The grant was dated, witness
Katherine, Queen of England, and General Ruler of the same,
at Westminster on the day named above.‡

The more distant portions of the possessions were granted to
Henry Lord Audley, William Gurle, Sir Martin Bowes, Chris-
topher Campion, John Rollesley, Richard Tate, John Pope,
Robert Curson, John Gates, William Bodye, John Small, Thomas
Goodwyn, Dominic Lomelyn, Robert Harrys, Richard Taverner,
and others. To pursue the history of these does not enter into

* Pat. 35 Hen. VIII. p. 9, mm. 14 (26), 13 (27). Orig. 35 Hen. VIII. p.
4, r. iiij˟ˣxv.

† Harl. Cart. 51 H. 21.

‡ Part. for Grants, William Grene. Pat. 36 Hen. VIII. p. 14, mm.
37(3)—34(6). Orig. 36 Hen. VIII. p. 5, r. l.

the scope of my subject, which ends with the dissolution of the House that owned them.

I have already informed the reader that no part of the ancient structure is now visible. It is said that masses of masonry yet exist below some of the neighbouring houses, and the memory of the Priory still lingers not only in the adjoining Church, but in the courts and offices which stand upon its site. Very sad it is to know that some of the most beautiful portions of the House were reserved for modern Vandalism needlessly and stupidly to destroy. " What remains to be said of the ancient crypt ?" asks Malcolm. " That it would not have required repair for 500 years to come. Had the enormous masses of fungous webs which depended from the arches of this beautiful work been carefully swept away, and the walls rubbed with a dry broom, the ancient windows reopened, the earth that clogged the pavement removed, and its other defilements cleared off, these crypts, now scattered in piles of rubbish, would have formed a church—how infinitely superior to forty I could name ! The regret with which I saw those slender pillars torn from their bases, and the strong, though delicate, arches sundered in masses, is still warm to my remembrance."*

To whom the disgrace of this barbarian act is to be attributed, the reader has no need to be informed. On the site, however, of one of the most interesting of the monastic remains of London, now stands one of the demurest of alleys in S. Helen's Place, and incomparably the ugliest of civic edifices in Leathersellers' Hall. THOMAS HUGO.

APPENDIX.

THE Constitutions of the Dean and Chapter of S. Paul's for the Nuns of S. Helen's are so interesting in themselves, and so valuable an addition to this class of documents, that my reader will probably be glad to possess a more exact transcript of them

* Malcolm, Lond. Rediv. iii. 562, 563.

than that which is furnished by any of the copies already printed.
So far as the press can represent its peculiarities, the original
runs as follows:

"Reynold Kentwode Dean and Chapeter' of the churche of
Poules to the Religious Women Prioresse and Couent of the
Priory of Seynt Eleyns of owre Patronage and Jurysdiccyoñ
inmediat and euery Nunne of the sayde Pryory gretyng in
god with desyre of Relygious obfuaunce and deuocyoñ ffor as
moche as in owre Visitacyoñ ordinarye in ȝowr' Priorye boothe
in the hedde and in the membris late actualy excersyd we haue
foundeñ many defautes and excesses the wiche nedyth notory
correccyoñ and reformacyoñ We wyllyng vertu to be cherysshed
and holy Relygioñ for to be kepte as in the rulee of ȝowre
ordyrre We ordeyñ and make certeyñ ordenauns and Jniunc-
cyoñs weche we sende ȝow Jwrete and seelyd vndir owr' comonne
seele for to be kepte in forme as thei ben articled and wretyñ
vn to ȝow

ffirste we ordeyne and Jnioyne ȝow that devyne fuyce be doñ
by ȝow duly nyth and day and silence duly kepte in due Tyme
and Place aftir' the obfuaunce of ȝowr' religioñ

Also we ordeyne an Jnioyne ȝow Prioresse and Couente and
eche of ȝow synglerly that ȝe make due and hole confessioñ to
the coffessor assigned be vs

Also we Jnioyne ȝow Pryoresse and Couent that ȝe ordeyne
conuenyent place of firmarye in the wiche ȝowre seeke sustres
may be honestly kepte and relevyd with the costes and expenses
of ȝowre house acustomed in the relygion duryng the tyme of
heere sekenesse

Also we Jnioyne ȝow Prioresse that ȝe kepe ȝowr' Dortor
and ly ther' Jnne by nyth aftyr obfuaunce of ȝowre religioñ with
owt that the case be suche that þe lawe and the obfuaunce of
ȝowre religioñ suffreth ȝow to do the contrarye

Also we ordeyne and Jnione ȝow Prioresse and Couent that
noo seculer' be lokkyd with Jnne the boundes of the cloyster' ne
noo seculer' psones come with Jnne aftyr the belle of complyñ
except wymment seruauntes and mayde childeryñ lerners Also
admitte noone soiornauntes wymment with owte lycense of vs

Also we ordeyne and Jnioyne ʒow Prioresse and Couent that
ʒe ne noone of ʒowre sustres vse nor haunte any place with
Jnne the Priory thorowgh the wich euel suspeccyoñ or sclaunder'
myth aryse wech places for certeyñ causes that move vs we
wryte not here Jnne in owr' psent Jniūccyoñ but wole notyfic
to ʒow Prioresse nor have no lokyng nor spectacles owte warde
thorght þe wiche ʒe myth falle in wordly dilectacyoñ

Also We ordeyne and Jnioyne ʒow Prioresse and Couent that
somme sadde woman and discrete of the seyde Religioñ honest
wele named be assigned to the shittyng of the Cloysters dorys
and kepyng of the keyeys that non psone have entre ne issu in
to the place aftyr complyñ belle nethir in noo other tyme be the
wiche the place may be disclaunderid in tyme comyng

Also We ordeyñ and Jnioyne ʒow Prioresse and Couent that
noo seculer' wymmeñ slepe be nyth with Jnne the Dorto⸢ with
oute speciall graunte had in the Chapell house among ʒow alle

Also We ordeyne and Jnioyne ʒow that noone of ʒow speke
ne comoñ with no seculer' psone ne sende ne reseyve lettes
myssyves or ʒeftes of any seculer' psone with oute lyccnce of the
Prioresse and that there be an other' of ʒowr' sustres psent
assigned be the Prioresse to here and recorde the honeste of
bothe ptyes in suche cōmynicacioñ And suche letters or ʒeftes
sent or reseyvyd may turne in to honeste and wurchepe and
none in to velanye ne disclaunderid of ʒowre honeste and
religioñ

Also We ordeyne and Jnione ʒow Prioresse and Couent that
noñ of ʒowre susters be admitted to nooñ office butt they that
be of gode name ꝉ fame

Also we ordeyne and Jnioyne ʒow that ʒe ordeyne and chese
on of ʒowre susters honest abille and Cunnyng of discrecyoñ
the which can may and schall have þe charge of techyng and
informacyoñ of ʒowre susters that ben vnkunnyng for to teche
hem here fuice and the rule of here religioñ

Also for as moche that diūce fees ppetuell corrodies and lyuers
have be grauntyd be for this tyme to diuerce officers of ʒowre
house and other' psones whech have hurt the house and be
cause of delapidacyoñ of the godys of ʒowre seyde house we

E

ordeyne and Jnioyne ȝow that ȝe reseyve noon officer' to noo
ppetueˡˡ ffee of office ne graunte noo annuete corody ne lyuery
with out speciaˡˡ assent of vs

Also we Jnioyne ȝow that aˡˡ daunsyng and reuelyng be
vtterely for borne among ȝow except Cristmasse and other
honest tymys of recreacyoñ among ȝowre selfe vsid in absence
of seculers in aˡˡ wyse

Also we Jnioyne ȝow Pᵒoresse that þere may be a doore at þᵉ
Nonnes quere that noo straungers may loke on them nor they
on þᵉ straungers wanne þei beñ at diuyne service   Also we
ordene and Jnione ȝow Prioresse þᵗ þᵉre be made a hach of
conabyˡˡ heyth crestyd wᵗ pykys of herne to fore þᵉ entre of
ȝowr' kechyñ þᵗ noo straunge pepiˡˡ may entr' wᵗ certeyne
Clekettꝑ avysid be ȝow and be ȝowr' Stward to suche psonys as
ȝow and hym thynk onest and conabyˡˡ

Also we Jnioyne ȝow Prioresse that non Nonnes have noo
keyes of þᵉ posterne doore that goth owte of the cloyster' in to
the churchȝerd but the Prioresse for þere is moche comyng in
and owte vn lefuˡˡ tymys

Also we ordeyne and Jnioyne that no Nonne have ne receyve
noo Schuldryñ wyth hem in to the howse forseyde but ȝyf that
þᵉ pˡite of þᵉ comonys turne to þᵉ vayle of þᵉ same howse

Thes ordenauns and Jniunccyons and iche of them as thei be
rehersid aboue We sende vnto ȝow Prioresse and Couent chardyng
and cōmaundyng ȝow and iche of ȝow alle to kepe hem truly
and holy in vertu of obedience and vp on peyn of contempte
And that ȝe doo them be redde and declared iiijᵒʳ tymes of the
ȝeere in ȝowre Chapeˡˡ [house] be fore ȝow that thei may be
hadde in mynde and kepte vndir peyne of excōicacyoñ and
other lawfuˡˡ peynes to be ȝove in to the psone of ȝow Prioresse
and in to singuler psones of the couent whech we purpose to vse
aȝens ȝow in case þᵗ ȝe dissobeye vs   Reservyng to vs and
owre successo'res powr' thes forsayde ordinnaunces and Jniũccyoñs
to chaunge declare adde and diminue and with hem despense
as ofte as þᵉ case requirith and it is nedfuˡˡ Jn to which witte-
nesse we sette owre comoñ seele ȝovyñ in owre Chapiˡˡ house
the xxj day of the Monyth of June the ȝere of owre lord Milˡiⁱmo

cccc^{mo}xxxix^{no} Et Anno r̄r̄' henrici sexti post conqm decimo
septimo *"
A fragment of the seal is appendant, of dark brown wax.
The document is of parchment, measuring 20½ inc. by 15 inc.
and is endorsed "Seint Poul," "sub altare x°," "Jniunccões
Sĉe Helene," and, in a much later hand, "Ordinances for regu-
lation of the Nunnes of St Helens, neere Bishopsgate, in
London."

Fastened to the upper left-hand corner is a small piece of the
same material, on which is written, in a hand of the thirteenth
century, a petition of the Prioress and Convent to the Dean,
Archdeacon, and others, in defence of some contested property
belonging to the Priory. The Prioress "D" was, I believe,
the first of those dignitaries; and the dean and archdeacon were
respectively Alardus de Burnham, Dean of S. Paul's, 1204—1216;
and Walter Fitzwalter, Archdeacon of London. The left edge
is injured, but the following will be found a not inaccurate copy
of a document, which, though hitherto unpublished, is of special
interest and importance to an historian of the earlier years of
the House:

"Viris Ven⁹ablibʒ. ℨ dn̄is. A. dec'. W. Archid'. Lundoñ. ℨ
Cel̃is coarbil̃s D. Humil̃. P⁰orissa. ℨ Conuent⁹ Ecclie Sĉe Helene
Sal̄ ℨ obedienc̄. Dil̃ci nob̄ in dño W. fundatoris nr̄i laboribʒ
ℨ angustiis quas p 9t°uersia coram vob̄ mota. M. fila syñ. sup
l̃ra. W. Wrhot .... dem irrogauit injuste. debita compassione
deferentes tam apllõi. q̄ᵃ phibicõi. p iure ℨ pos[sessio]ne nr̄a a.
nob̄ inl̃põitis renūciam⁹. volentes. ℨ concedñtes. vt jux* formā
9pmissi. inl̃ ptes pecdet arbil̃u. Malum⁹. q^d si oportũit carere
fundo. q̄ᵃ amico. spantes. nicĥomin⁹. de justicia [vr̄]a q' indemp-
nitati Ecclie nr̄e q*ntû sedm̄ dm̄ pol̃itis. eritis puisuri. Val̄t."

T. H.